unexpected Gifts

TO JENNIFER BRIAN.

May you be blessed with unexpected GIFTS.

LOVE (PEACE and JOY

Leslie Neale
Dane

zofia monika dove

unexpected gifts

forever books
WINNIPEG, CANADA
www.foreverbooks.ca

Unexpected Gifts

ISBN: 978-1-926718-12-5

Cover Design: Yvonne Parks Design
Book Design: Andrew Mackay
Managing Editor: Rick Johnson
Editor: Kelly Dvorak

www.unexpectedgifts.ca

Published by

Forever Books

WINNIPEG CANADA
www.foreverbooks.ca

Dedication

To the power that makes my heart beat, the power which allows everything to grow, move and unfold. For the freedom of choice that this power extends to me in every given moment of my life.

To my parents, my first teachers, for showing me what true presence and absence is.

To my mom – for her unconditional love, and to my father – for his care and protection.

To my children, whose love and presence was at times the sole reason for my perseverance.

To my best friend Anna, who has always stayed by my side

To my true friends: you are the most beautiful flowers on the path of my life.

To Bianka my friend, for allowing me to stay by your side until the very end of your journey. The end of your life began my purposeful living.

To Ann my dear, elderly friend, for being my Canadian mother, for showering me with your love and wisdom.

To my patients, especially the elderly and gravely ill people who over many years, welcomed me into their most personal spaces and shared their understanding of life with me.

To all who had and have access to my heart, they were and are my biggest teachers.

To every moment of awareness that Love is
and endures forever.

Table of Contents

Preface

In the spring of 2006, I worked at Grace Hospital in Winnipeg, Canada. I had a friendly conversation with one of my patients, Audrey, during a typical physiotherapy session and before I knew it, I was reading an article she had written. Her story was about the importance of hugs in our lives and the impact that hugs have on us. That article struck a chord deep within me.

I remember standing there, trying to describe to Audrey how odd I felt. I'd never experienced that particular feeling and struggled very hard to communicate how my thoughts were gathering in a new, never-experienced way.

I said to Audrey, "I'm feeling inspired." My describing my feeling and state of being as "inspired" came as a surprise to me. Today, I realize that Audrey's article gave me the spark that ignited my writing.

To my total astonishment, I wrote my first poem two days later. From childhood, some people dream of becoming doctors or firefighters, but I must confess that in my wildest dreams, I never imagined or wished to become a writer, especially a poet. The larger surprise is that English is my second language.

Immediately after writing my first poem, I felt very enthusiastic and called Audrey to read it to her. Audrey's reaction to my big news was somewhat unexpected. I knew she was happy for me, yet she didn't seem to be surprised that I'd written a poem.

The following days and months brought many magical moments as I kept writing poems. Four years have passed since that first inspirational moment by Audrey's bedside. I continue to write.

In my younger years, I had no interest in poetry and if

I'd been invited to a poetry reading, I'm sure I would have found a polite way to excuse myself from attending. Therefore, I am especially thankful, as well as surprised, that people have taken the time to listen to my poems.

Right from the beginning of my writing, I had this unstoppable, heartfelt desire to share my poetry with others. I started with my family, friends, and then my patients, many of whom were elderly, often gravely ill people.

My patients were my first and best critics. By their reactions, I realized they often experienced the most amazing insights while listening to my poetry. Many of them opened up and shared their most profound thoughts and feelings, which they connected with through my writing. That in itself was inspirational and triggered further writing. I will forever be grateful to those people for validating my written words.

My patients were the first ones to encourage me to share my poetry with other people. I took their advice and stepped way out of my comfort zone and began reading my poetry to whoever would listen. I shared it at my lawyer's office, during bank appointments, and even at the dentist's office (after he was done with my teeth, of course).

I volunteered to read my poetry to patients on geriatric and psychiatric wards. St. Boniface Hospital honoured me with an invitation to share my writing with patients, family and staff members at the beautiful Buhler Art Gallery, which, at the time, was hosting an exhibit from the National Art Gallery entitled La Rue/The Street.

Over time, I began to share my poetry with audiences in various public places: open mike events in local bookstores, nursing homes, assistive living residences, churches, even pubs. To my ongoing surprise, the audiences listened in silence and later offered encouraging feedback. Many asked for copies of my poetry.

Eventually, my friend and I made pamphlets of my poems, which disappeared in no time. The doors of opportunity kept opening. It felt as though the poetry itself was taking me on an amazing journey, a journey for which I had never bargained.

I was invited to speak on a local Polish radio program and at events dedicated to victims, veterans and survivors of the Second World War. My poems were published by the Addictions Foundation of Manitoba, by both Grace and St. Boniface Hospitals, and by Cancer Care Manitoba. Even the Polish newspaper Czas published one of my poems, which was written in English.

Many times fear, doubt and apprehension tried to stop me, but true to the promise given to my dying patients, I persevered and never refused an opportunity. My audiences consisted of children, teens, adults and the elderly, professors involved in teaching writing, physicians, and even psychologists. I read my poetry to Ukrainian, Polish, Native, Italian, and French people for whom English was a second language. Sometimes I received harsh criticism, but that only taught me new lessons about myself and my writing. I am thankful for each experience.

The initial strong advice from my patients, as well as the ongoing interest in my writing, convinced me that I should publish this book. At the beginning of my journey, I promised myself that if I ever published my poetry, it would be under my maiden name, and only when my divorce became finalized. Guess what! Two weeks after I received my final divorce papers, a patient's niece tracked me down to see if my book had been published yet.

You see, that elderly woman's vision gradually

worsened and eventually she was unable to read. Instead, she asked her niece to read aloud to her. When I heard that, I was reminded that many of my patients had enjoyed listening to my voice and the way I read my poems.

Many of my patients also had trouble with vision and it was suggested that I consider producing a CD of my poetry. That way, those with vision difficulties could enjoy listening to the poems instead of reading them. So, after receiving all these cues, I started the process of publishing...

Kelly was my neighbour but in no time we became best friends. Not only was she my main supporter in the hardest times of my life, but she also became the editor of my poetry. Eventually, Kelly and her family moved to Saskatchewan and I thought that perhaps life was taking us apart for good, but I was wrong. Kelly invited my children and me for a visit the following Christmas. How could I pass up the invitation?

On the morning of Christmas Day, at -40C, I found myself driving west to visit Kelly and her family in Saskatchewan. Never mind that they entertained and fed us, Kelly also found time to type and edit twenty of my poems.

Fortunately, Kelly and her family returned to Winnipeg for a short stay and during that time she edited the rest of my poems. I am unable to count the days and hours this woman spent with me typing, spacing and editing my writing. In addition, she didn't charge a penny. I am forever grateful for all the time and help she gave me during her busy life.

I cannot forget to mention Gus Henne from Forever Book Publishing House. Gus is a trustworthy, knowledgeable, and experienced man in the business of publishing. His selfless advice was a priceless gift. He helped me envision the whole process and pointed out important nuances in the process of publishing a book. Words cannot express how thankful I am for all your help, Gus.

Many other people, whom I call "angels", were also involved. You each know who you are. The encouragement of my angels is what influenced me to finish this project. I am thankful for each of my angels, who unexpectedly appeared at just the right times in my life, and for all the help and advice that they gave me. This book is a wish that came through.

Enjoy *Unexpected Gifts*.

Zofia Monika Dove

1. Do You Have a Minute to be Present?

Hello! How are you this morning?
　You do ask me every day
　Do you really want my answer?
　Do you really want my say?

Look into my eyes
Look into my face

　Do you really want to know
　All my troubles
　All my sorrows
　That my heart must undergo?

Stop and listen
Stop and hear me

　Hear my voice - its tone and flow
　Watch my body language, posture
　They will tell you
　They sure know

　Do you really have a minute
　To be present and to hear?

How sincere is your question?
How concerned are you, sir?

Yet the question that you ask me
Every morning on your way
　Makes me feel already noticed
　It could truly make my day!

2. To Enjoy and to Take Care

Dedicated to Bianka

We've watched life going away
We wished the candle's glow would stay
But it wasn't meant to be
It was fading, we could see

What was actually taking place?
I've been deeply asking grace
Somehow subconsciously I knew
There is a lesson in this too

Now I know how precious is
That my heart answers my wish
When I wish to run it goes
When I wish to stop it slows

Now I know how precious is
My lungs filling with fresh air
I don't have to wish for that
Oxygen just fills them up

Now I know how precious is
When my head can go in peace
For a restful, sleep-filled night
Gets me ready for the next light

Now I know how precious is every minute I have here
I intend to take good care and enjoy what is here for me
Every beat, and every breath
Every word you say to me

I intend to take good care,
Before my candle burns away.

3. The Seed of Life

When I arrived to you in a bundle
The way you received me was so humble

I heard your promise said right there
That you will take the best of care

      And as you promised you've stood always near it
      And as you promised you've cherished my spirit

You answered to my demand at time
You knew it wasn't such a crime
    Yet somehow silently you did
    Plant in me the most precious seed

You cried at times, when watched my choice
You knew, no point to raise your voice
    Yet somehow patiently you did
    Plant in me the most precious seed

What kind of thank you can I say?
For the richness of my heart today?
I'll share this gift, in whole at least some
              That deepest love
                  You gave me
                     Mom.

4. Misplaced Mother's Tears

She lost a loved one not long ago
It stopped her life's flow
She wonders why she's unable to cry
Over her lost child
 She often fears: Where are my tears?

No one can see them or peek
She feels very lonely
They are buried inside very deep
She guards them strongly

She lost her child, it was abrupt
The pain is blocked and trapped
She keeps her child inside
Plays the past in her mind
 She often fears: Where are my tears?

They want to come out and surface
She guards them strongly
They wish to come down her cheek and face
She holds them fondly

If you could help her and show
She has the need and right to now
How to find the way to let go
Allow her tears to flow

 Maybe rather than keeping her tears trapped
 She could hold her dear child
 Only in her heart.

5. They're Here to Teach Me

Angels were sent to me holding some light
To touch me inside and cheer up my heart

Five angels were sent from heaven into my arms
They travelled to me straight from the stars

> Sometimes they scream
> Sometimes they fight
> > Nevertheless, they're angels to stay by
> > my side

They love me truly
Their love is deep
They love me when I'm healthy or sick
They love me when I'm happy or sad
They love me even when I get mad

> They love me always for just being me ...

When I stop, watch, listen ... then I can see

Their arrival was full of purpose and well thought of
> They came here to teach me
> unconditional love
> They came here to teach me that heart mat-
> ters the most
They're in the forms of my children, *not* unseen
ghosts.

6. I'm More Than a Ladybug

Don't preach me rules
You can't live by
Don't tell me I can't reach the sky

I do believe, I do have trust
My only role is Love – an absolute must

To love you, whoever you are
If you are homeless
If you are a star

To love myself, whoever I am
If I'm trustworthy
If I'm in shame

I do believe, I do have trust
My only role is love – an absolute must

To love you regardless of what you've done
Acquired titles
Or reached for none

To love myself regardless of what I've done
Noble and big things
Or hardly some

Don't preach me rules you can't live by
Don't tell me I am not
Innocent and free like a ladybug
Wrapped in the sun's love, feeling so snug.

7. A Part of True Love

I never thought life would turn out that way
I know you're thinking, "It's easy for me to say."
  If you only knew what I've been through
  To be able to say this to you

I'm certain in my heart – I know I tried my best
I never imagined life would show me this quest
  On this part of the way, which I choose to turn to and
  walk on
  You can't stay by my side, you meant to continue on
  your own

    I can't keep you and protect you
    Somehow I know
    It is important: You have to experience life to
    grow

    I can't escape this thought
    Somehow I know
    It is inevitable, once you've gone through the
    worst, you'll know

    I can't stop it or change it
    Somehow I know
    It's the only chance for you to learn flow

Flow easier throughout the rest of your life
With the true love and peace
For that love I'll stay on my knees
It is hard for me to do it, yet
Somehow I know
There is true love in letting you go.

8. For the Peace of Our Minds

I am ready to forgive
  Not to forget
All the experiences while by your side

  I am ready to forgive you for the peace of your mind

I am ready to forgive
  Not to forget
All the troubles I willingly went into
  I didn't take time to anticipate

I am ready to forgive
  Not to forget
The good moments
  I didn't know how to appreciate

I am ready to forgive
  Not to forget
The methods that weren't always noble
  I didn't know how to communicate

I am ready to forgive
  Not to forget
That I should have been true to my heart
  Not to simulate

I am ready to forgive
  Not to forget
All the experiences while by your side

I am ready to forgive myself for the peace of my mind.

9. Blocks to Creative Thoughts

When I look inside you what do I see?

Frantic restlessness
Dreadful unhappiness
Problems you anticipate
Worries ... will you recuperate?

What is the point of fearful worries?
What is the point of dwelling on stories?

Tomorrow hasn't arrived yet
You haven't even taken that step
All you need to take care of is now
All you have is this moment in time

When I look inside you, what do I see?

Regret-filled sadness
Resentful madness
Dwelling on what you can't undo
Problems you've been through

What is the point to endless, "so sorry"
What is the point to constant worry?

Yesterday is in the past
Leave it behind, forget your loss
All you need to take care of is now
Allow yourself a moment in time

Put your heart at ease
Let the worrying cease
All it does is builds blocks
And stops creative thoughts

It drags and pulls you down, unable to enjoy what's now.

10. The Tool of Your Lips

One day I had a chance to hear your voice
And you spoke in such a special way

The soft, kind word you spoke, an almost
    insignificant one,
Carries power like a strong drum
Echoes in my mind for many days
It's not only how you said it, but what it says

The quiet nice word you spoke, an almost
    insignificant one,
Carries energy, like a gentle chime
Resonates in my mind for many days
It's not only how you said it, but what it says

It contains special meaning once placed in my
    heart and mind
It says I'm good ... special ... worthy ... even
    smart and kind.

I used words ... I don't want to say too much
They didn't have that special touch
They were cutting, like a sharp blade
I'm the only one to blame
I did choose them, what a shame.

I choose not to use them now

Who can stop me, if I choose?
To use nice words, the same like yours
With that touching special balm
    With that soft uplifting calm

One day I had the chance to hear your voice
And you spoke in such a special way
      Now I know that I can choose
      To do the same.

11. A Gift You Could Volunteer

I'm sitting here, I'm waiting for you
I wonder if you will enter my space
Guided by some unexplained faith
I wonder if you will bring me a hug
Rather than a common shoulder shrug

I'm lying in bed, I'm waiting for you
I wonder if you will enter my space
Guided by some unexplained grace
I wonder if you will bring me a smile
I haven't seen a real one for a while

I'm standing here, I'm waiting for you
I wonder if you will enter my space
Guided by some unexplained chance
I wonder if you will bring me a tap on my shoulder
It could warm up my heart that gets colder

I'm waiting still I'm always here
I wonder if you have a moment to spare
If you will bring: A kiss on my head
                       A rub on my back
                       A moment of patience
                       A simple handshake

                       It has potential to uplift me or break
                       me

I've been that one that never could see
How deeply touching kindness can be.

12. Have the Guts to Trust

If I didn't trust the moment
    Where would I be?
I would miss all the treasures
    That life presents to me

    A smile on my child's face
    Renewed, slower life pace
    Reflection of the rising sun
    And the feeling that life can be fun

    The beauty of a peaceful sky
    New friend that entered my life
    A chance I'm given once more
    With widely opening door

    An inspiring word you speak
    A child's inquisitive peek
    A phone call I'm meant to get
    And laughter I almost forget

If I didn't trust the moment
    Where would I be?
I would miss all the joy and love
    That life presents to me.

13. In the Very Early Morning

It's Sunday morning
I wake up, it's still dark
Nothing is rushing me, nowhere that I have to run
Then I will sit here for a change, I will welcome the sun

This peace is amazing
    It touches my soul
Some say it is boring
It's not at all dull

It is somehow expressive
    Almost as if it's confirming to me
That I should stay in one spot
That's the way to be

This peace is uplifting
    The air stays so still
Nothing disturbs the stillness
    Not even a cat
        He usually wakes me up with meowing, that brat

In the moment of quietness
    I think briefly of those
Who can't enjoy peace like this
    Live with fright and chaos

And then I feel very thankful
To whoever or whatever makes this peace
I am not too religious
Yet I feel it puts me at ease

Drifting back to that peace, I stay still on my seat
And I think to myself – it is joy, it is neat.

14. While in Her Way

A strange woman appeared, surrounded in the darkness
  She looked frightened and very hopeless
  She approached me on the spot - right there
  I must admit I was so scared

She explained to me what had happened
  I was so doubtful if I should trust her
  She looked so helpless and very scared
  I had the means to help, if I dared

      I was so puzzled, I was not sure
      If her words were honest, true, pure
      I didn't have much time to decide
      She was pleading to be taken to the Light

I could have left her
I could have said:
  "I'm rushing,
     I'm sorry,
         It's a busy day."

I didn't know if her words were pure
If I could trust her for sure

    Then I remembered
    I was once her
    Uncertain, frightened, the world was unfair

    Then I remembered
    I was once her
    Searching for help, in a state of despair

The darkness used to wrap around me
Someone did share, dared to help me

I knew that instant
I understood
I'm put in her way, 'cause I can choose

Guide her to the lit spot where all fear fades
It took just a minute
I knew that darkness – I was once in it.

15. Your Silver Hair Offers Gold

Silver, silver, silver hair
Now I see you everywhere
Now I do slow down on my walk
       Sit down near you, listen and talk

       Your trembling voice sends message, clear
       My point doesn't travel in noisy scream

       Your aging signs – brown spots on the skin
       Shows me true beauty lies within

       Your wrinkled skin on arms and face
       Reminds me – my life also runs its course
       in its own pace

       Your giving heart taught me such
       True treasures are not in what I touch

Your wisdom acquired throughout your journey
Is meant to spare me some troubles, surely
Your silver hair offers life's gold
So why was I so oblivious and cold?
       What made me run past you, ignore … ?
       Teach me how to get through life's storms
       to peaceful shore.

16. To Put on the Shelf

When you were a toddler, a child
    I tried my best
I tried to provide gentle guidance
    Not force you to rest

    I let you fall, then get up
    Allowed you to experience life's way

    I knew the dance would not always be smooth
    You went through some grooves

    Sometimes you struggled then thrived
    I stayed by your side

        I never kept you in one spot
        For the sake that you wouldn't break

When I'm old and sick
    I hope you'll do your best
All I need is support when I'm weak
    Don't force me to rest

    Perhaps all I need is a loving one by my side
    To be a tactful guide

    Perhaps all I want is you, to stand near
    To offer a listening ear

    Perhaps all I need is you to let me struggle then thrive
    Just stay nearby

        Please don't place me on a fixed shelf
        Where you think I'm safe

Please consider my voice
Allow me my choice
Please let me live my life,
It still goes on until I'm gone.

17. Dying Used to Frighten Me

When I met him, he looked weak
Had a hard time to breathe or speak

I asked him to participate
He complied, just for my sake
So I could follow the routine
Yet the struggle that I've seen ...

He knew that there was not much of a point
No treatment could restore his joint
No way, it would make him any stronger
It just kept him here, to suffer longer

It is his right, it is his choice
Sit up, stand and use his voice

He wants to say ciao, goodbye, goodnight
How can we take away this right?

He is ready, who are we to say
He must stay and suffer another day
Play the game by the rules we make ...
– Let him go, for goodness sake.

His achievements done and gone
He is ready to go on
He knows truly, he is smart
It's his choice to leave and part

I can tell he's not confused
Neither by drugs or by booze

If the support is withdrawn
He would stay just on his own
He knew the outcome, he was sure
His life, he could no more endure

I could tell he was all with it
His mind ready, so his spirit
He wants to say ciao, goodbye, goodnight
Can we deny him such a right?

At the end someone heard him and made the decision
There will be no more pills, no incision
Once the support was withdrawn
He stayed shortly on his own.

He was mindful, noble man.

Wrapped up all his business here,
Then said thanks for being near

Used the rest of time with loved ones to speak aside
There was no dry eye, we all cried.

An understanding came upon me
That I had a very rare chance to see
Once you have a fulfilling life
Passing could be a peaceful sight.

18. Droplets

The droplets were falling slow
From every direction that I've ever known
Every one came on time, landed deep
I couldn't run away from them or skip

The droplets were timely, it wasn't a chance
They would not allow me to live in the same trance
Every one brought its message, made me think
If I continued on the same course, I would only sink

The awakening had happened to me
Because my spirit was meant to be free
Wasn't meant to be suppressed and kept in a cage
Such a treatment is certain to trigger some rage

The next chapter is up to me to write
If only the guidance sustains by my side
I received special tool, I can't afford to lose
I hope the page stays open so I can use
The gift that I was presented for free
Which was the understanding that made me to see
That everything is different, nothing is the same
I was allowed to enter another life game

The awakening had happened to me
Because my spirit was meant to be free
Was meant to be loved, cherished every day
Such assurance is certain to keep me on the right way

My heart's deep desire is answered at last
I need to stay tuned, so it would not pass
I hope the droplets will continue to appear
So one day I can say: "I am completely free, without
fear."

19. My heart Needs Time

There was a time I believed I had loved
And my heart was so trusting and open wide
It was trying so many times different ways
It was used, tricked, lied to - ugly sight.

    You love me, you tell me now
    You ask me to return the same
    But my heart is still freshly wounded,
    It needs time to heal and get sane

There was a time I believed I was loved
And my heart had its gate open wide
It was pouring all the love that it could
It was stabbed many times - very hard

    You love me, you tell me now
    You ask me to return the same
    But my heart is still freshly emptied,
    It needs time to learn to trust again

There was a time I believed in love
And my heart still desires true one
But it is cautious, testing, and watchful
Yet hopeful that the real one will come.

20. It's a Cool Place

I am in a place which no eye can see
I am in a place where everyone is meant to be
I am in a place where everything makes sense
    Where nothing goes by chance
    Where my heart is ready
    Where the course is steady
    Where everything is clear
    Which doesn't know fear

    Where everything is just
    With no existing 'must'
    Which is filled with joy
    Where no one needs toy
    Where there is no soon or late
    When no one has a mate

    Where there is no time
    Where boredom is crime
    Where everyone can get it all
    Where no one is too small
    Where everyone is put at ease
    Where all desires cease

Everyone has the right to hear the guiding voice
Everyone has the right to use their choice
Everyone has the right to find the key
Everyone has the right to come here and see

This place has many different names
I hope you'll read ten clues and take a chance
To find this cool place.

21. Are You to Live For?

One would say it was serendipity
Another that it was faith
Someone else would think of it as an interesting case

I don't know, maybe it was meant to be
I guess I have to live on and perhaps I'll see

Who gave you permission to appear on my way?
Who gave you permission to stand there that day?
Who gave you the knowledge to speak the right phrase?
Which unknowingly to you made me stop in a daze?

Who gave you the permission to unlock my heart?
Who gave you the permission to trigger a new start?
Who gave you the knowledge where to find the right key?
Which unlocked my heart so easily then set it so free?

Who gave you permission to open the door?
You maybe the one to live for?

22. The Power of Thought

There is way more here for me
Than your naked eye can see

I am following my dream
It's not triggered by a sin

There is thought behind my action
You could say I'm on a mission

The light is green, it's only fair
I'm taking time to thoroughly prepare

My intention stays the same
Regardless of what you say
It will not weaken my strength,
It does not matter what you think

The presumption is on you
The conclusion that you drew
Is a product of your thought
Will not change the way I talk

There is way more here for me
Than your naked eye can see

I will try and try again
As long as it won't cause pain
As long as its meant to be
The result will come, you'll see

Impossible is nothing, dear
Something whispers to my ear

Don't you try to stop me now,
I'm determined, my dear pal
I feel this internal need,
I'll try hard – I might succeed

I will not be stopped by fear
I'll pursue my dream, it's near
If I gave up, never tried,
I could waste my entire life.

23. To Admit

Far on horizon I saw lightning, still far away,
A sign of storm coming my way
Distant yet clear thunder wanted to say
To look for shelter, a safe place to stay

I didn't take it seriously
I turned away to pretend
That the strong winds couldn't bring
Very serious event

I saw the thunderstorm coming
There were visible signs
I heard the thunderstorm coming
There were warning sounds

All I did – I looked to hide under a tree
Hoping to stay safe and dry there
To put it lightly – this was very silly of me

It was in the fury of tearing winds
In the most frightening phase
An out-of-control, spinning craze

It was only when I admitted to my ignorance
When I took the blame for being wrong
That I got gutsy, and became strong

I took action
I walked out from underneath that tree
Found real shelter
And with that, a sea of calmness for me

If there are clear warning signs
Of a storm coming your way
They're meant to guide you to safety
To ignore them means to take a chance, to become prey.

24. Come Closer to the Gate

In the room of loneliness you still stay
You don't talk about it, you won't say
How lonely, scared, and unhappy you are,
How everyone seems distant and far

In the room of loneliness you're still unaware
There is a simple way out
You're almost at the end of the rope
You're ready to scream and shout

    No one can open the gate
       and help you out
    No one can stop this misery,
       your shout

    You're the one that needs to take
    the first step
    You're the one that can open the gate
    for help

You seem to be so far into the loneliness,
You're almost blind, unable to see that help IS
This help is waiting for a very long time
You dwell in your thoughts on pride or crime

With this help all will fade, go away
The promising help knows the right way
It's reaching out, knows what's at stake
It's your freedom, LIBERTY, for goodness sake!

The promising one loves you with all his heart
Can see you still carrying bright spark

No one can open the door
And help you out
No one can stop this misery,
your shout

You're the one that needs to make
the first step
You're the one that can open the door
for help

Give it a try and trust
come closer to the gate
All it takes is to push it a little ajar
Before you know, you'll shine like a star

I hope you'll use this information
and reach true peace and inspiration.

25. Bring the Best Out of Me

Perhaps the change starts with me

When I drift off the main track, get lost
                              Wait for me

When I give up on myself
                              Believe in me

When I'm crushed and down
                              Comfort me

When I struggle with decisions
                              Guide me

When I need time to see
                              Stand by me

Does the change start with me?
It's not just about me.
One day, I will mirror all I see
One day, I will mirror all you do.
Bring the best out of you.

26. Motionless Fall

When I first wake up
So much is going on

I'm in the world
I've never been before

I'm confused, scared
Don't recognize
        this place
        this face
        your face
        my face

They tell me what to do
They show me what to do

I am emotionless, numb, going insane

Anger
Anger
Fills me up
With one snap,
        All this trap

Friends are gone – another blow
How come I'm the one to show?

How can I willingly go through it all
Without your help
        I can't break
            Motionless Fall.

27. My True Side

In my troubles and strong lure
I stayed honest, I stayed pure

In my sickness, dreadful pain
I held tightly to stay sane

In my sorrow and despair
I still trusted one would care

In my darkness and great fright
I kept hope for smallest light

Through acceptance found at night
    I discovered my true side
Clenched to it with all my might
    My true integrity inside.

28. Restlessness

When my heart is near by yours, I am certain
 I am ready to reveal, drop the curtain

When we talk and you are near
 My fear seems to disappear

When I'm close, you hold my hands
 Calmness surrounds us, that's the sense

When I listen, hear your voice
 It seems clear, I know the right choice

 Regardless of all of that, when we're apart

I battle some kind of doubt
 I consider pulling out

My thoughts rush me to a quick answer
 It's weakening me, like some cancer

Part of me wants to stay, other run
 Should I hold back, or have fun?

I am restless, I am searching
 Should I let go, or keep clenching?

 Am I to compromise and self-adjust? Is this
 the way to build trust?

29. Life's Finesse

If I claim that you're mine
                    I could use you
If I hold you too tight
                    I could lose you
If I speak on your behalf
                    I silence your voice

I can't make you stay or go – that's your choice

It's illusion when I say
                    I'll always stay
It's illusion when I claim
                    For the rest of the way
It's illusion when I think
                    We couldn't drift apart

No one makes me stay or go - that's my right

It's life's virtue
            True finesse
                    We don't belong or possess

            One can go on or stay still
            That's free will.

30. Intrigued

Faces – that's what I want to see
Faces – that's what I like to observe
   To watch what makes them calm
      Or gets on their nerve

Faces, which tell more than they intend
   Which use disguise and pretend

Faces, that push you away, invite to come near
   That are profoundly sad, yet shed no tear

Faces, that burst with happiness, seem not to worry
   Which are apologizing, yet don't seem sorry

Faces, which say "I miss you" before you're gone
   Peaceful, satisfied faces, ready for dawn

I'm glad I simply see them,
The privilege to observe them intrigues me
And I wonder how would it be

      If they all disappeared,
                  Or I couldn't see?

31. Journey

As I was driving my car
I spotted a falling star
It took me back to a comment
I used to make in such a moment

I looked back
    through the rear-view mirror
    I took a glance
    into my past trance

I saw the places I drove through
All the right, wrong turns I took
I carefully observed and looked
At:
    What I've done
    What I've thought
    What I've said
Created either good fortune or bad

I saw patterns in my past behavior
And I realized I'm my own good fortune creator

    Through the rear-view mirror,
    I took a glance
    into my past tense

I saw patterns in my past behavior
And I realized I'm my own bad luck creator

I looked forward
  The road was leading to new dimension
  It required my attention
  It asked for wise decision
  To avoid further collision

I knew from the past
Careless driving creates dust
While carefully driving my car
Can get me to promising star

Not just the one I saw ahead

In the reflection of what I've been through
In the reflection of the rear-view
  I saw something else
  I saw rising light
  To promising new day's start.

32. Wide Spectrum

I've learned about a wide spectrum
Of waves in my early days

Some I can hear, others I see
Some are undetectable to you and me
There are those heard only by animals
And specific to birds with sharper vision
And those protecting junctions from collision
Amongst many are the micro, that cook
And others that give shivers – can spook

It occurred to me, it can actually be
That people are on different wavelengths, as you and me

From the position of my wave, I have a different view
I don't detect the sounds you do
I'm unable to see from your perspective
Therefore I have a different objective
Since I'm on a different wavelength
I ought to go with my wave's strength
Stay with my current and flow
In order to move to the next wave and grow

How does one move to a higher wave?
Obtain a wider view?

Through work on self and acceptance of you.

33. How Ironic

The smell of cigarettes
The fragrance of your perfume
Music played to our ears
That is over too soon

      Brings the thought of you ...

    How barely I understood
    How hardly I knew
    Who you were
    When you were here

My thoughts come to impasse ...
    Cannot encompass the gifts you brought ....

    How ironic
These weren't the times with gin and tonic

It's only with the last breath, which brought your death

    That surely I knew
    Truly understood
    Who you were
    When you were still here.

34. Remained Present

The house fully prepared for happy life
    All that hard work could bring was there
    Except the well-known, typical *her*

Fancy clothes, full of hope, hanging on for special func-
tion
Yet the biggest hope was normal organ function
Pointless to look for her charm and chic
Pain was written on one's smiling cheek
No need to reveal yesterday's glowing skin
Mature reflection marked time running thin

The air in the room not like baby's breath
But suffocating with sentence of death

The permission to visit was given often
The silence was eerie, gave glimpse of the coffin

Tiny speck of her from yesterday
Was the only beauty of each day
With all that surrounding gruesome cloud
She stayed proud
Balanced
No sign of hysteria
Regardless of 'final days' criteria

To many in the midst of all this
It would be hard to find *her*
Yet privileged, I did
Not in her speech or size
She remained strong and present,
                    only in her eyes.

35. Harvest of Life

Unimaginable horror your young heart went through
There was nothing you could do
There was nothing you could have done different
Not your fault - you froze up, had stiff hand

Unimaginable terror and fear
     No wonder you turned a deaf ear
     No wonder you let your mind shut
With such a painful, deep, senseless cut
     I marvel how you survived,
     I wonder how you prevailed,
Wound inflicted with such a sharp nail?

How could you go on, and rise up,
How did you escape the darkness trap?

In your story of horror, of pain,
Lies examples of how to stay sane
How through hope life gathers its crop
Truth and love
     They rise always to the top.

36. Blind Love

I'll pick you up whenever I can
Even when I'm viewed as insane

I'll pick you up from clean place, or dirt
With broken heart, in stained or white shirt

I'll pick you up at any cost
In love with you, I get lost

To accept you, I'll use any measure,
'cuz you are my biggest treasure

I worry about you day and night
When you're not in view, out of sight

Without you days have just a dim light,
For you, I'll take on any fight

I know you are a psychopath, honey
In pursuing you, I'll spend my whole life,

    dear money.

37. No Time

No one has time to listen
No one has time to listen

No one has time to hear
     has time to hear

No one has time to feel
          time to feel

I wish
I wish

I hope
I hope

That time would stop
No chance would pass by
There would be no time.

38. With Ticking Clock

Pretending word came to me
Suggesting everything is as it should be
The lying word thought it was cool
The untrue story was very sure
That it was able to manipulate and lure

      My heart

        It tucked away its pain
        Giving new chance again
        Yet the lie chipped at my heart
        Challenging new start

Misleading word came again to me
And I pretended everything is as it should be
The dishonest word thought it was smart

        Yet again it chipped at my heart
        Challenging new start

I still remember the overwhelming shock
How lies can change any heart to rock
How little by little my heart was chipped at

      Instead

Of being filled with truth
That gives any caring heart a boost

How little by little was depleted of trust
That every heart to possess must

        If it is expected to be touched to the core and
        love more.

39. Just Average

I'm walking today
I enjoy it, hon

I had days I couldn't run
I had days I couldn't get up

Never mind *'get'* –
I couldn't *look* up

I'm walking today, I stay upright
I look ahead, I enjoy the sights

I'm walking now at normal pace
I carry around a content face

No need to take part in any *race*
No point to take part in any *craze*

Steady is Good
Average is GRACE

I'm walking today
I enjoy this pace

This is the one for me to embrace.

40. Locked Inside

When I looked at your doormat, I stopped
I read the sign on it, and my chin dropped
The word on it was facing the door
Rather than welcoming the visitor

And if you must know the truth
I thought the one that reversed it must be a silly goose

What I perceived as wrong
Was actually very right
That turned around doormat
Shone on my day a new light

The welcome sign at the door was putting down all the
fences
Suddenly I was open, and eager to take on new chances
The doubtful feeling was lifted
With just the change of my thought
New hope for coming events was brought

And very shortly after, an opportunity arrived
I tried and missed a few times, before I won and thrived

It's not the trying and failing
That is the biggest sin
But staying still, doubtful, and locked within.

41. Entitlement to Learn

Comfortable spot at life's table I had
But something came to my head
That I would like to change this seat
It wasn't because of my sore feet

I fixed my eyes on table's head chair
I worked for it, sweat, lost some hair
Eventually I sat down in this perfect spot
Now it will be fun - that's what I thought

But life was already preparing a plot

At first I was hinted to leave that place
That was the moment to save my face
Then life assured me it's only fair
For me to sit in a different chair

But I worked hard for it, I felt entitled
I had the right to hold to the title

Because of my pride and strong objection
Life, the one that knows true perfection
Removed me from out of there
By ejecting me from that chair

What initially appeared to me as life's rejection
Actually led to self-correction
Only with time, I came to learn
All are life's gifts
       ...I never earned.

42. Blank Check

Its ugly stage now
I can't deny
Another test
At times I cry

It's dirty and painful
    Shades mostly gray

It needs to get ugly
Before renewal
I need to remember
Life is not cruel

It's a matter of patience
    It's a matter of trust

I've seen it before
After loss comes gain
Life's understanding
Is paid for by pain

There's no such thing
Like life's blank check
        I either pay it forward
           or, I pay it back.

43. Come Back Future Change

'Change' – I thought I'm at ease with you
    Regardless if you come slow or fast
I can be friends with you, 'change'
    Leave old times in the past

And yet deep need
Pulled me back in time

Was it a blessing, curse, or crime?

Now I dwell in
        If?
           Maybe?
           and Why?

My lips full of laughter
Mixed with weeping eye

Wondering 'if only' steals the precious 'now'

'Change' – to your blessings now I humbly bow
'Change' – my friend please come back
           slow, or perhaps fast
With you, I'll move forward, I will not be covered in dust
I understand you now 'past', you were the required base
On which 'change' will build –
           but at its own pace.

44. Thank You

For the moment in his strong arms
    That have no right to make change

For dark sigh, bright eyes

For feeling his once unspoiled heart
    Unable to stay by its beat

For touching, voiced thoughts
    Not destined for me to keep

For whispering lips
    No longer meant to unite

For stillness of the air
    Grounded night

For moment engraved in hearts
    That is gone, yet captured

For the weakness of love
and
The strength of letting go.

45. While Sinking

Out of respect of your love
I do not disclose
Can't solve
   your dilemma

Out of protection of your emotion
I do not step
Into commotion
   your view

time
experience
thinking
with that, the hope

that when you're sinking
you'll turn for confirmation
for yours and others peace.

46. Unavoidable

I sensed it would come
I would be fool
Thinking that life would change the rule

Only for me
Only for you

'Just a stage,' the wise say, 'You are not through'

I knew it would come
You knew it too
I dread the thought of parting with you

Or like you say, 'Just a short space apart' –
'Next to' when we consider law of the heart

It is as you say, 'All for the better'
In pain or free time – drop in, write a letter

Time to explore new, open sea
Stay you cannot, I clearly see

Now I experience what the wise ones predicted
That even with obeying, life's rules will be still inflicted.

47. In Us

We were true once
Do you recall?
That magic call?

We knew whatever
The future endeavors
Sure what will follow
Will not be hollow

We knew it once

The knowing faded
The brightness shaded
Then we cross-traded
With that degraded

So many times

We were pure once
I do recall
It is still here
Inside us all.

48. Passive Silence

Good fortune
Sent me an angel to help me out
Instead of talking, I used shout
Other times, I created tension
Through lack of cooperation

     Or, to my convenience
     I used silence

Good fortune
Sent me the truest friend
But rather than thank you or smile,
I watched my friend from a distant mile

     Of my observation
     Without appreciation
     With no justification
     Of my friend's intention

Passively using my best friend
The kind that only heaven can send

     I almost lost you
     I almost did
All the time thinking of my, not your, need

     And rather than speak up and convey
I chose passive silence and had nothing to say.

49. In The Absence

When world revolved
   Around my hurt
When I was fighting
   For bread and shirt

You were alone
Waiting for me
I'm sorry baby
I could not see

How in my absence
   I caused you pain
How quick and easy
   Love went to drain

No one to cheer you at performing site
No one to tuck you in, kiss you goodnight

My absence, baby, caused you much fear
I'm sorry honey, I was not near

Now in your absence,
   I guess it's fair
I'm feeling lonely
   Is your heart there?

To resume beat
Go strong and steady
Please give me a chance
When you are ready

Let's talk, do something
Don't wait for fate

I hope for one chance
Please, don't be done
I beg you, baby
Forgive me, son.

50. Magic of Your Name

A close one to you came to announce
Name I am learning how to pronounce

We've never met, yet you're not a stranger
You bring with you peace, not danger

The word about you just hardly passed
Yet you already lent the best cast

To embrace your new heartbeat
    I must admit is very neat

Now I reflect,
             rethink,
                    restate.
Take back the words that I still can take
I again smile, give friendly shake

I do it for your love, name's sake.

Always believe in your heart's magic
When the world tries to impose its logic
When rules will try to trap you in a box
Find your way out, like a skillful fox

You're not here yet, a mystery to us,
Your name brings magic, don't let it pass.

51. Do You Suppose I Can Be Like Her, Father?

Young and beautiful
Could have been a glamour girl
Or like the French say, "Un Professeur"
I was there, I'm the witness to her talent
She was once mine, and I was her friend

Young and promising
This is what the world had seen
Until it all spun into an obscene scene
The pain she was unaware about
Through needle pokes, changed her to a dropout

Young and pure
The world couldn't know
The courage that my friend had shown
When asked to share her medication
Shocked me with 'NO' - left in frustration

Young and dying
As the world would predict
And I am screaming inside in conflict
'Cause comments made about apparently wasted life
Stab my heart like a knife

Her courageous refusal to share
Was my life's pivotal point, I swear

Do you suppose I could be like her and help other
in the midst of my deep suffering, Father?

52. Special Event

We arrived in one place
Some brought pain, others stories were tragic

We never bargained for upcoming magic

One brought acceptance
    Understanding other
    Openness by most
        Not just by the event's host

Willingness was present
Pairing with imagination
Of being in another's situation

Forgiveness surfaced
However intended for a Receiver
Touched all, calmed heart of the Giver

Embracing at last
Quenched one's need for belonging
Brushed off on all heart's longing

Innocent trust
Not rigid anticipation
Added to richness of that day's creation

Throughout the event
Oblivious to all
These elements gently
Were composing One

True Unity

Submerged in love and joy
Which replaced an old fun.

53. Return to the Plan

Deep, deep pain in my heart
    Can't explain why
Tears land on the paper
    I again cry

Over lost promise
Over crushed dream
My heart is aching
I want to scream

At times I worry
At times I hate
Sometimes I fear
That I lose faith

At once I surrender
    Trust in life's plan
Peace sets in my heart
    Renewed – I can.

54. Unrecognized

You came close to me
Could not come closer, honey
Our arms brushed
Yet you did not recognize me ... funny

Disturbed, outside I rushed

Frantic search for something lost
Was coming day's cost
Fogging in my mind
Then struggle to find

Way back

Slowly inside I returned

Could not come closer, honey
Approached it gradually ... funny
And discovered
Through an act of contrition

That primary is: self-recognition.

55. An Infection

You can't see this infection
It doesn't give a rash
It eats you up
Silent one – hush, hush

You can't see this wound
It doesn't appear –
Toxic mix of suspicion and fear

It's contagious, honey
Once you're exposed to it
You can't easily get rid of it

It lingers inside
Causes headaches, splits hairs
Asks a question, another one
                    ... then more

You're observing, wondering why or what for
You're always questioning
Another's intention

This is the result of manipulation.

56. One

The tiniest
    droplet of pure love
        splashed nearby

The tiniest
    speck of it
        landed inside

... Everything mattered no more

      Just one did ...
      One second
      One word
      One breath
      One look
      One step

      One.

57. Indescribable

Would you let go?

Of the abbreviation, or lack of it, in front of your name
The predictability of the setting from which you came
Protection by those whose kiss uplifts you
All that your mind knew, when you knew.

Would you dive?
Vulnerable, no sword

Would you arrive?
In the name of a given word

No belongings or belonging to
No sounds to express your view
No place you could call home
No memory where you came from

Would you take a chance?
To dance with the unknown
Become indescribable, yet drawn
Led, like the blind that came
All in the name, one name.

Which is the power of one beat
So your life would become truthful and complete.

58. In Preparation

They stood firm, withheld times of deep freeze
To observer, life within them *did* freeze

    Motionless, without outside help
    Some bent to the ground
    Part of them broken
    Silent, never outspoken

They stayed still, withstood the seasons of death
With the end of each came new breath

    At last, awaited day arrived
    With life giving wind, they thrived
    Moved, danced, became the main focus,
    Had been given attention, like fresh crocus

After the final death season
Arrives ultimate life force

    Old trees know that through
    Experience of seasons, of course.

59. Purification

If I had a choice I would never choose
To take it easy and snooze

To attend to smooth surface — no scars
Life would be a shallow farce

With the loss of grip on my senses
I began to grasp what life's sense is

Through purification of my heart
Came the end, then ... amazing start

So I would respond to your touch
Sparks in your eyes spoke so much

So my beat can meld into yours ...
For that I would never change past course.

60. Insiders Know

I am on my way to a place
I have never seen
I just heard some talking
From those that have been close to it

Or others that truly entered
Spent time within
Never came across same
Grumpy or grim

Lightness
Acceptance
Calmness
       in their hearts
Gentleness
      in their voices
      and body parts

Ever since they have been there
They know what's at store
So they call on this magic place for

Clear guidance
 Protection
 Every cure

Those that have been there at least once know
They live with trust, in hope and glow.

61. All You Need

You look so peaceful when
        In the sun
Everything is ...
        Nothing needs be done
Submerged in profound moment
No motion needed, no comment

You look so radiant when
        In the peace
Comfort is
        No burden, no fees
No chatter, wants, uncertainties
Dual or plural identities

You are aware, that's all you need
Like sprouting, new seed.

62. Would I

It's like the times by your home
   in your garden

I close my eyes
   and still see the sun

I cover my ears
   yet hear distant bell

I lie on a fresh grass
   like then, there
    familiar beat in the air

Light fluffs drifting by
   carrying invitation on blue sky

'Would you follow?'

   ... Nothing will stop me this time.

63. Before

I felt you
  Before touch
I knew your voice
  Before words
I longed for you
  Before contentment
I met you
  Before arrival
I was yours
  Before
    I

64. I'm Longing For

Unintentional word .... for seeing
Unnoticeable strength .... for being
Distance .... with no means of measure
Indescribable expression .... of pleasure

I'm longing
   For the kind of reflection
   That appears without projection

I'm longing

   To be that open.

65. Eruption

The ray is white; it comes straight to pierce
In this state, there are no fears

The white ray erupted

Colors dance in a new dimension
Freeing love feels great,
                    may I mention!

66. I Looked for It Too Far

I felt it once in my life
I failed to recognize
It's always waiting for me
So eager to revitalize

It is hard to comprehend
It is always waiting for me
Extending its helpful hand

When you are down
When you are desperate
When no one seems to care

That love is always waiting
I dare you to turn to her

When you are scared
When you are lonely
When no one seems to share

That love is always waiting
I dare you to turn to her

It's pure, uplifting, calling
It never wants to judge
It's clear, untainted, ... Holy

This love is the One and Only
It's present everywhere
I looked for it all over
It's near me, it's right here.

About the Author

Zofia was born behind the "iron curtain" in socialist Poland where over ninety percent of the population was Roman Catholic. That was one of the many paradoxes she encountered in her life. She married in 1980 and two years later, at twenty, she became a first-time mother of her only Polish-born child.

Zofia became a physiotherapist in 1986 and found employment in one of Poland's two largest rehabilitation centres. Although her professional career was highly satisfying and proved to be the right choice of occupation for Zofia, the young family of three experienced many challenges due to the political and socio-economic realities of Poland in late 70s and 80s.

Against her family's advice, Zofia's husband escaped from Poland in 1986, eventually arriving in Winnipeg, Manitoba, Canada. Due to miraculous circumstances, Zofia was able to join him just one and a half years after his escape, immigrating to Canada in 1987.

Nothing could prepare the new immigrants for the challenges that lay ahead. At times their youthful enthusiasm ran thin. The need for knowledge of the language was underestimated by both as neither Zofia nor her husband spoke English. The language barrier played a critical role in their settling in their new reality.

It was hard to find employment, to make friends outside of the Polish community, and to access government support services. Zofia's Polish credentials were not recognized. Professional training was out of the question at that time because of Zofia's non-existent English language skills, lack of funds, her feeling like an outsider, and her insecurities.

However, good fortune seemed to be at work. With the help of newly found Polish friends, Zofia was able to enter a Basic English course and in May, 1989, she started employment with one of Winnipeg's local hospitals as an occupational therapy technician. That began a new chapter of her life – her career in the Canadian Health Care System as a rehabilitation technician, a job which she enjoys to this day. Last year marked Zofia's twentieth anniversary in Canada's rehabilitation services.

Over the years, the family expanded with three new additions. Today, Zofia is the proud, single mother of three sons and a daughter.

Both her love of service to her patients, along with raising her four children brings Zofia an immense sense of satisfaction. She is proud of her contribution to the multicultural and multi-religious society in her new home – Canada.

In 2006, Zofia became a student at the University of Winnipeg and her life took another unexpected turn. While working with a patient, Zofia was inspired to start writing poetry in English. She never intended to be a writer, especially not a poet.

A new chapter now unfolds as she journeys with her poetry. Life is full of surprises. One never knows what waits around the corner. But one thing is certain with Zofia: there's never a dull moment!

An Invitation

It is only through the heart's own deep recognition, that light can start shining from and into ... allowing for the natural flow of love to take place.

No one knows all, and all do not know The One, yet it is through open sharing that we can be one.

It is my hope that through sharing this poetry, you, my reader, will find yourself receiving unexpected gifts in whatever form they may have come to you.

If these written words affected you in any way, please do not hesitate to share this with me.

I welcome you to contact me by email at zofia@unexpectedgifts.ca or through my website at www.unexpectedgifts.ca